THE STENCIL COLLECTION
Seashore Desi
Denise Westcott Taylor

Seashells **8**

Dolphins & Mosaics **12**

Nautical Knots **20**

Coral Reef **24**

Treasure Islands **16**

Rock Pools **28**

INTRODUCING STENCILLING

O nce you begin stencilling you will be amazed at the wonderful results you can obtain quite easily and without spending a great deal of money. This book introduces six themed projects and provides ready-to-use stencils that can be used with numerous variations in design – just follow the step-by-step features and simple instructions. With very little paint and only a few pieces of equipment you can achieve stunning results. Have fun!

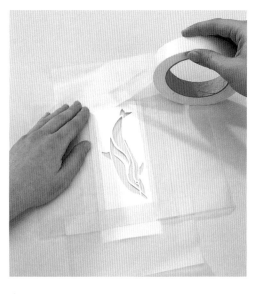

BASIC MATERIALS

Paints and Decorative Finishes
Emulsion paint
Water-based stencil paint
Oil sticks
Acrylic paints (bottles and tubes)
Specialist paints (for fabrics, ceramics, glass etc)
Spray paints
Metallic acrylic artists' colours (gold, silver etc)
Silver and gold art flow pens
Bronze powders (various metallics)
Gilt wax

Brushes and Applicators
Art brushes (variety of sizes)
Stencil brushes (small, medium and large)
Sponge applicators
Mini-roller and tray

Other Equipment
Set square
Blotting paper
Scissors or scalpel (or craft knife)
Roll of lining paper (for practising)
Eraser
Soft pencil
Fine-tip permanent pen
Chalk or Chalkline and powdered chalk
Long rigid ruler
Tape measure
Plumbline
Spirit level
Low-tack masking tape
Spray adhesive
Tracing paper
Paint dishes or palettes
Cloths
Kitchen roll
White spirit
Stencil plastic or card
Cotton buds
Methylated spirits

CUTTING OUT STENCILS
The stencils at the back of the book are all designed to be used separately or together to create many different pattern combinations. Cut along the dotted lines of the individual stencils and make sure you transfer the reference code onto each one with a permanent pen. Carefully remove the cut-out pieces of the stencil. Apply 50 mm (2 in) strips of tracing paper around the edges using masking tape; this will help to prevent smudging paint onto your surface.

REPAIRING STENCILS
Stencils may become damaged and torn from mishandling, or if the cutouts have not been removed carefully, but they are easy to repair. Keeping the stencil perfectly flat, cover both sides of the tear with masking tape. Then carefully remove any excess tape with a scalpel.

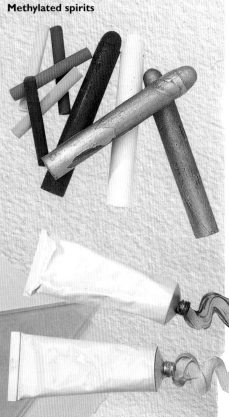

GETTING STARTED

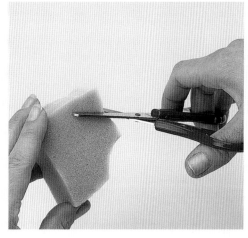

DUPLICATING STENCILS

Stencil plastic (Mylar) can be used; or card wiped over with linseed oil, which left to dry will harden and make the surface waterproof. Place the cut-out stencil on top. Trace around carefully with a permanent pen inside the cut-out shapes. Cut along the lines with a scalpel and remove the pieces. You may prefer to trace on top of the design, then transfer your tracing onto card.

MAKING A SPONGE APPLICATOR

Sponging your stencil is one of the easiest methods, but you may prefer to use a stencil brush, especially for fine detail. Using a piece of upholstery foam or very dense bath sponge, cut pieces 12–50 mm ($\frac{1}{2}$–2 in) wide and approximately 50 mm (2 in) long. Hold the four corners together and secure with tape to form a pad. You can also round off the ends with scissors or a scalpel and trim to a smooth finish. The small-ended applicators can be used for tiny, intricate patterns.

HOW TO USE WATER-BASED PAINT

Water-based paints are easy and economical to use and have the advantage of drying quickly. For professional-looking stencils, do not load your sponge or brush too heavily or you will not achieve a soft, shaded finish. Paint that is too watery will seep under the stencil edges and smudge. If the paint is too heavy you will obtain a heavy block effect rather than the soft stippling you require.

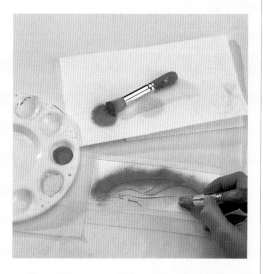

LOOKING AFTER STENCILS

Stencils have a long life if cared for correctly. Before cleaning make sure you remove any tape or tracing paper that has been added. Remove any excess paint before it dries, and wipe the stencil with a damp cloth every time you use it. If water or acrylic paint has dried and hardened, soften it with water and ease it off gently with a scalpel. Then use a small amount of methylated spirits on a cloth to remove the rest. An oil-based paint can simply be removed by wiping over the stencil with white spirit on a cloth. Stencils should be dried thoroughly before storing flat between sheets of greaseproof paper.

HOW TO USE OIL STICKS

Oil sticks may seem expensive, but in fact go a long way. They take longer to dry, allowing you to blend colours very effectively. Oil sticks are applied with a stencil brush and you need to have a different brush for each colour. Break the seal as instructed on the stick and rub a patch of the colour onto a palette, allowing space to blend colours. As the stencil sticks dry slowly, you need to lift the stencil off cleanly, and replace to continue the pattern.

PRACTISING PAINTING STENCILS

Roll out some lining paper onto a table and select the stencil you wish to practise with. Using spray adhesive, lightly spray the back of your stencil and place it into position on the paper. Prepare your paint on a palette. Dab your sponge or brush into the paint and offload excess paint onto scrap paper. Apply colour over the stencil in a light coat to create an even stippled effect. You can always stencil on a little more paint if a stronger effect is needed, but if you over apply it in the first place it is very difficult to remove. Keep separate sponges for different colours.

PLANNING YOUR DESIGN

Before starting to stencil take time to plan your design. Decide where you want to use the patterns, then work out how to position the stencils so that the design will fit around obstacles such as doorways and corners. The techniques shown here will help you to undertake the job with a systematic approach.

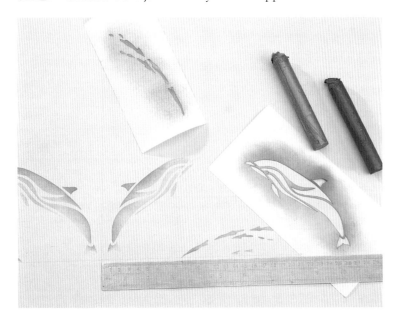

PUTTING PATTERN PIECES TOGETHER

1 Before you apply your design, stencil a sample onto lining paper. Mark the centre and baseline of the design on the paper and put together your pattern pieces. You can then work out the size of the design, how it will fit into the space available and the distance required between repeats.

2 You can avoid stencilling around a corner by working out the number of pattern repeats needed, and allowing extra space either between repeats or within the pattern. Creating vertical lines through the pattern will allow you to stretch it evenly.

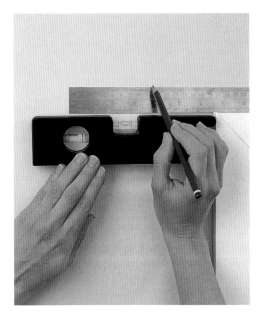

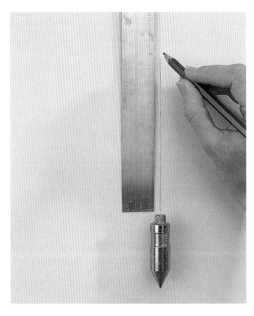

MARKING BASELINES AND HORIZONTAL LINES

Select your stencil area, and take a measure from the ceiling, doorframe, window or edging, bearing in mind the depth of your stencil. Using a spirit level, mark out a horizontal line. You can then extend this by using a chalkline or long ruler with chalk or soft pencil.

MARKING VERTICAL LINES

If you need to work out the vertical position for a stencil, hang a plumbline above the stencilling area and use a ruler to draw a vertical line with chalk or a soft pencil. You will need to use this method when creating an all-over wallpaper design.

FIXING THE STENCIL INTO PLACE

Lightly spray the back of the stencil with spray adhesive, then put it in position and smooth it down carefully. You can use low-tack masking tape if you prefer, but take care not to damage the surface to be stencilled; keep the whole stencil flat to prevent paint seeping underneath.

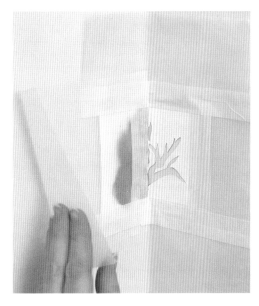

MARKING THE STENCIL FOR A PATTERN REPEAT

Attach a border of tracing paper to each edge of the stencil. Position the next pattern and overlap the tracing paper onto the previous design, tracing over the edge of it. By matching the tracing with the previous pattern as you work along you will be able to align and repeat the stencil at the same intervals.

COPING WITH CORNERS

Stencil around corners after you have finished the rest of the design, having measured to leave the correct space for the corner pattern before you do so. Then bend the stencil into the corner and mask off one side of it. Stencil the open side and allow the paint to dry, then mask off this half and stencil the other part to complete the design.

MASKING OFF PART OF A STENCIL

Use low-tack masking tape to mask out small or intricate areas of stencil. You can also use ordinary masking tape, but remove excess stickiness first by peeling it on and off your skin or a cloth once or twice. To block off inside shapes and large areas, cut out pieces of tracing paper to the appropriate size and fix them on top with spray adhesive.

MITRING STENCIL PATTERNS

1 When you are stencilling a continuous pattern and need to make a corner, mask off the stencil by marking a 45-degree angle at both ends of the stencil with a permanent pen. Mask along this line with a piece of masking tape or tracing paper.

2 Make sure the baselines of the stencil on both sides of the corner are the same distance from the edge, and that they cross at the corner. Put the diagonal end of the stencil right into the corner and apply the paint. Turn the stencil sideways to align the other diagonal end of the stencil and turn the corner.

PAINT EFFECTS

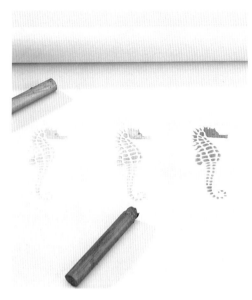

CHOOSING COLOURS

Take care to choose appropriate colours to create the effect you want. Stencil a practice piece onto paper and try a variation of colours to ensure you are pleased with the result. Different colours can make a design look entirely different. Use spray adhesive to fix your practice paper onto the surface on which you wish to produce the design so that you can assess its effect before applying the stencil.

APPLYING WATER-BASED COLOURS

Water-based paint dries quickly, so it tends to layer rather than blend. It is best applied by using a swirling movement or gently dabbing, depending on the finished effect you wish to create. Once you have applied a light base colour, you can add a darker edge for shading. Alternatively, leave some of the stencil bare and add a different tone to that area to obtain a shaded or highlighted appearance.

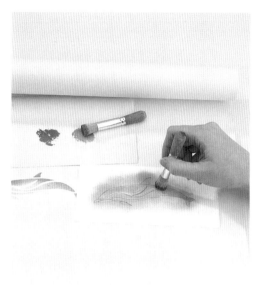

BLENDING OIL-STICK COLOURS

Oil sticks mix together smoothly and are perfect for blending colours. Place the colours separately on your palette and mix them with white to obtain a variety of tones or blend them together to create new colours. You can also blend by applying one coat into another with a stippling motion while stencilling. Blending looks most effective when applying a pale base coat, then shading on top with a darker colour.

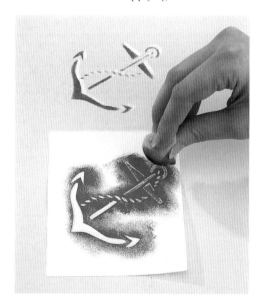

HIGHLIGHTING

A simple way to add highlighting to your design is first to paint in your stencil in a light tone of your main colour, then carefully lift the stencil and move it down a fraction. Then stencil in a darker shade; this leaves the highlighted areas around the top edges of the pattern.

GILDING

After painting your stencil use gold to highlight the edges. Load a fine art brush with gold acrylic paint and carefully outline the top edges of the pattern. Use one quick brush stroke for each pattern repeat, keeping in the same direction. Other methods are to blow bronze powder onto the wet paint, draw around the pattern with a gold flow pen, or smudge on gilt wax cream, then buff to a high sheen.

APPLYING SPRAY PAINTS

Spray paints are ideal on glass, wood, metal, plastic and ceramic surfaces. They are quick to apply and fast drying, but cannot be blended, although you can achieve subtle shaded effects. Apply the paint in several thin coats. Mask off a large area around the design to protect it from the spray, which tends to drift. Try to use sprays out of doors or in a well-ventilated area. Some spray paints are non-toxic, making them ideal for children's furniture.

DIFFERENT SURFACES

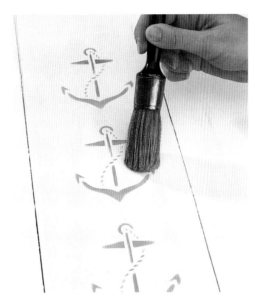

BARE WOOD

Rub the wood surface down to a smooth finish. Then fix the stencil in place and paint with a thin base coat of white, so that the stencil colours will stand out well when applied. Leave the stencil in place and allow to dry thoroughly, then apply your stencil colours in the normal way. When completely dry you can apply a coat of light wax or varnish to protect your stencil.

PAINTED WOOD

If you are painting wood or medium-density fibreboard (MDF) prior to stencilling, seal it with a coat of acrylic primer before adding a base coat of emulsion or acrylic paint. If the base coat is dark, stencil a thin coat of white paint on top. Apply your stencil and, if required, protect with a coat of clear varnish when it is completely dry.

FABRIC

Use special fabric paint for stencilling on fabric and follow the manufacturer's instructions carefully. Place card or blotting paper behind the fabric while working and keep the material taut. If you are painting a dark fabric, best results are achieved by stencilling first with white or a lighter shade. Heat seal the design following the manufacturer's instructions.

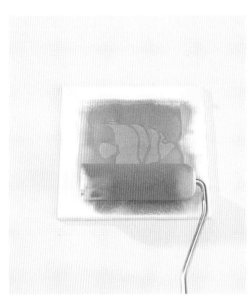

CERAMICS

Use special ceramic paints to work directly onto glazed ceramic tiles, and unglazed ceramics such as terracotta. Make sure all surfaces are clean, so that the stencils can be fixed easily. Apply the paint with a brush, sponge, spray or mini-roller. Ceramic paints are durable and washable, and full manufacturer's instructions are given on the container.

GLASS

Before applying the stencil make sure the glass is clean, spray on a light coat of adhesive and place the stencil in position. Spray on water-based or ceramic paint, remove the stencil and allow to dry. If you wish to stencil drinking glasses, use special non-toxic and water-resistant glass paints. An etched-glass look with stencils on windows, doors and mirrors can be achieved with a variety of materials.

PAINTED SURFACES

Stencils can be applied to surfaces painted with matt, satin or vinyl silk emulsion, oil scumble glazes, acrylic glazes and varnishes, and to matt wallpaper. If you wish to decorate a gloss surface, stencil first with an acrylic primer, leave to dry and then stencil the colours on top. Surfaces to be stencilled need to be smooth so that the stencil can lay flat.

SEASHELLS

The seashell theme in this light and airy bathroom will help make a great start to any morning. The shell border interspersed with watery splashes sits just above the wood panelling, painted blue with touches of lilac. More shells are painted on the shelf above. To avoid the border looking too repetitive, paint the shells in a random order. You might decorate other items in the room with single shells for a co-ordinated look, or trying stencilling with fabric paints on a blind or curtains.

PAINT COLOUR GUIDE

White   Lilac   Powder Blue

CO-ORDINATING THE BATHROOM COLOURS

1 Paint the timber cladding with blue emulsion and the wall above with white emulsion. Mix a glaze using acrylic scumble and blue paint and use this to lightly colourwash the wall.

2 Stencil the shells in a random design interspersed with the splash stencil G to make a border at dado height. Use blue and the lilac paint for a three-dimensional effect.

3 Paint the shells that appear to be resting on the shelf in blue paint. Finally, give the stencils and the timber cladding a protective coat of varnish.

PROJECT PATTERN

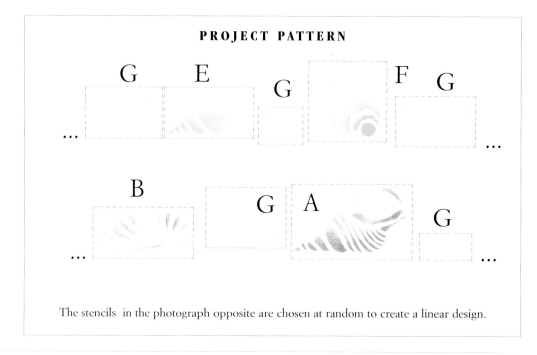

The stencils in the photograph opposite are chosen at random to create a linear design.

GETTING THE BORDER LEVEL
Fix a piece of thread horizontally on the wall. Mark a line on each stencil with a pencil, then carefully match this stencil line to the thread. In this way the stencils can all be placed at the same level.

PAINTING THE SPLASHES
There is no need to paint the whole stencil – here just parts of the splash stencil G have been used between the shells. Cover the sections you are not using with masking tape. Try turning and flipping individual splash marks for variety.

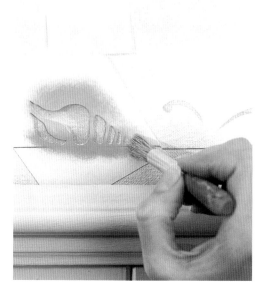

ADDING SHADING TO THE SHELLS
Paint the shells with blue paint. Then mix a little lilac with the blue and use this darker colour to paint the top and bottom edges of the stencil. This will give the shape depth and make the shell look rounded.

SEASHELL VARIATIONS

Shells can be arranged as a border or painted singly. Put them together in patterns or a circle. They would make a pretty edging for a small table or tray. Combine them with the ribbon (stencil D) for a softer effect. Here they are painted in tones of blue, lilac and aqua, but try other soft colours for a completely different look. Pastel greens or pink and peach would also work well.

SCALLOPS BORDER (STENCIL C)

RIGHT: WAVE BORDER (STENCIL G)

OYSTERS AND RIBBONS FRIEZE (STENCILS F AND D)

PAIRED SHELL HEARTS (STENCIL B)

**LEFT: SPLASH STRIPE
(STENCIL G)**

**SMALL SHELLS EDGING
(STENCIL E)**

LARGE SHELLS GROUP (STENCIL A)

SPLASH SPRAY BORDER (STENCIL G)

SHELL CIRCLE (STENCIL E)

SIMPLE LARGE SHELLS BORDER (STENCIL A)

REFLECTED SHELLS BORDER (STENCIL B)

BELOW: OYSTER BORDER (STENCIL F)

TWINING RIBBONS PATTERN (STENCIL D)

DOLPHINS & MOSAICS

Inspired by Roman mosaics, this dolphin stencil makes a beautiful border for a bathroom floor. The dolphins swim around the room between a double mosaic edging. Here you can see just a corner of the floor but the whole design creates a peaceful, relaxing bathroom. Try using different colours. Terracotta adds warmth, but paint the mosaics without this colour if you want a fresher and cooler effect. You can easily plan curves and circular patterns from this versatile set of stencils.

PAINT COLOUR GUIDE

Terracotta	Sea green	Cream
Pale blue-green	Deep blue-green	

PAINTING A ROMAN-STYLE FLOOR

1 Prepare the surface of the floor thoroughly so that it is clean and even. Apply at least two coats of cream paint to the floor. Paint the walls with pale blue-green paint.

2 Stencil the dolphins using deep blue-grey for their backs and sea green for their undersides. This gives them more dimension and makes them look more naturalistic.

3 Use all the colours in a random pattern for the mosaic tesserae around the edge of the floor. Use a mask to overlay individual tiles and separate colours. Varnish the floor to protect the surface.

PROJECT PATTERN

This arrangement shows how to plan the design around a corner as shown in the photograph opposite.

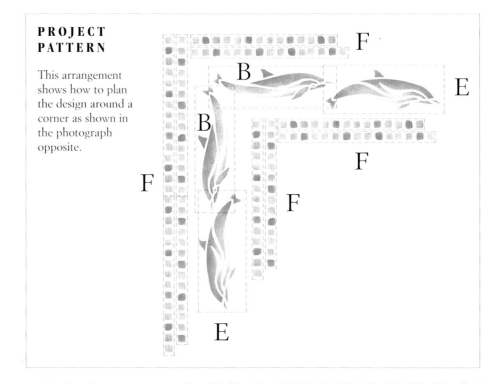

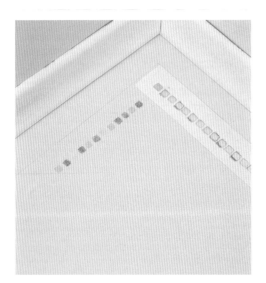

WORKING ROUND A CORNER

Decide on the layout of your design and mark the positions of the stencils using a soft pencil or chalkline. When working round a corner, line up the edge of the stencil to the mark and overlap the last painted tile.

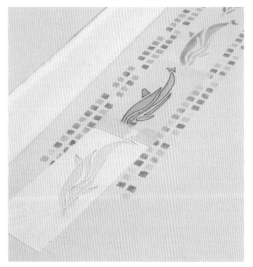

PAINTING THE DOLPHINS

Use dolphin stencils B and E for the border. Leave one stencil in place and attach a piece of tracing paper so that it covers the other dolphin. Trace over the design and use the tracing to register accurate repeats.

VARNISHING THE FINAL EFFECT

It is essential to varnish floor stencils to protect your work. At least three coats will be needed. A water-based floor varnish dries quickly and although it has a white, even bluish appearance when wet it will dry with a clear finish.

DOLPHINS & MOSAICS VARIATIONS

H ere are some ideas of the many ways in which this set of stencils can be used. You can make no end of frames, blocks or borders with the mosaic tesserae stencil F, experimenting with different colours and shadings. Use the splash stencil D for curved borders or circles. Mask out part of the wave stencil A for different sea conditions. Turn a child's bedroom into a dolphinarium!

WAVE BORDER (STENCIL A)

DOLPHIN AND SPLASH MOTIF (STENCILS C AND D)

CURLING DOLPHINS (STENCIL C)

TWO DOLPHINS MOTIF (STENCIL E)

DOLPHINS FRIEZE (STENCIL B)

ABOVE: REVOLVING DOLPHINS (STENCIL C)

LEFT: SEASPRAY BORDER (STENCIL D)

MOSAIC AND WAVE EDGING (STENCILS A AND F)

SPLASH (STENCIL **D**)

WAVE CORNER
(STENCIL **A**)

DOLPHINS TILE
PATTERN
(STENCIL **B**)

RIGHT: DOLPHINS CORNER
(STENCIL **C**)

MOSAIC TILES (STENCIL **F**)

DOLPHINS BORDER (STENCILS **B** AND **E**)

WAVE AND MOSAICS BORDER (STENCILS **A** AND **F**)

RIPPLE SPLASH BORDER
(STENCIL **D**)

TREASURE ISLANDS

Desert islands, stormy seas, treasure chests and pirate ships! Every little adventurer needs a place to store collected treasures and where better than this toy chest and set of boxes? The bright colours are perfect for a child's room and the treasure islands theme will stimulate their imagination and might even encourage them to be tidy! The designs have been painted as repeating patterns here, but you could easily put them together to make a picture or simple mural.

PAINT COLOUR GUIDE

Electric blue	Lemon yellow
Cherry red	Warm yellow

CREATING A TREASURE ISLANDS PLAYROOM

1 Paint the walls with a warm yellow emulsion. Mark the position of the dado and stencil the rolling waves stencil F around the room.

2 Give the large toy box a base coat of electric blue paint. Mark the positions for the outline flag stencil D, painting the flags alternately red and yellow. Add the skull and crossbones.

3 Paint the round boxes and small chest with the red, yellow and blue paints. Position the ship, waves, islands and treasure chest stencils around them as you wish and paint them with contrasting colours.

PROJECT PATTERN

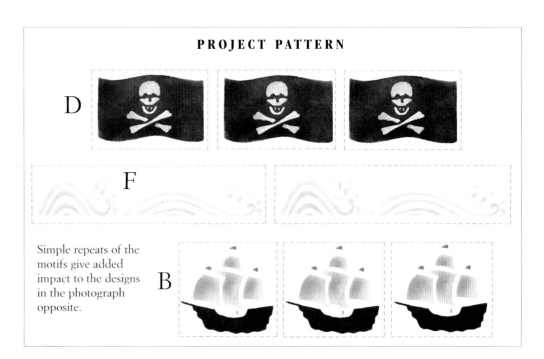

Simple repeats of the motifs give added impact to the designs in the photograph opposite.

STENCILLING ON A CURVED SURFACE
Measure the circumference of the box and divide by the width of the stencil to calculate the number of stencil repeats. You may need to adjust the spacing for the final stencil to fit perfectly into the space that is left.

MAKING THE STENCIL STAND OUT
When you are stencilling onto a strong-coloured background you need either to undercoat the design with white or, as here, to paint the stencil twice. This will give a greater depth of colour and brightness.

PAINTING THE PIRATE FLAG
Stencil D consists of two parts. First paint the flag and then, without moving the outline stencil, insert the inner part containing the skull and crossbones and paint in a contrasting colour. This flag has been coloured red and yellow rather than the traditional black and white.

TREASURE ISLANDS VARIATIONS

Although this set of stencils will appeal to children it is possible to adapt them for more sophisticated tastes. The rolling waves produce attractive flowing designs when they are reversed and the flags can be painted in other colours without the skull and crossbones to make a festive border. The ripples (stencil C) would add a delicate touch to a bathroom if painted in pastel colours.

WAVES MOTIF (STENCIL F)

PALMS AND RIPPLES EDGING (STENCILS C AND E)

SHIPS AND WAVES (STENCILS B AND F)

DESERT ISLAND FRIEZE (STENCIL E)

WAVES FRIEZE (STENCIL F)

RIGHT: WAVES CORNER (STENCIL F)

**LEFT: WAVES BORDER
(STENCIL F)**

PIRATE SHIPS BORDER (STENCIL B)

ABOVE: OVERLAPPING WAVES DESIGN (STENCIL F)

ABOVE: SIMPLE FLAG BORDER (STENCIL D)

TREASURE CHESTS FRIEZE (STENCIL A)

**FLAG BORDER
(STENCIL D)**

RIPPLE CORNER (STENCIL C)

NAUTICAL KNOTS

Rich burgundy walls make a stunning background for these strong rope nautical stencil designs, creating a room that looks smart as well as functional. Simple but stylish, the rope and knots, painted in shades of grey, frame the wall tiles. The tiles are decorated in silver with compass and anchor motifs. These versatile stencils look best in contrasting hues. Navy blue on a white wall or cream on terracotta would give a traditional classic look.

PAINT COLOUR GUIDE

Burgundy   Grey   Silver ceramic paint

White   Black

DECORATING THE SPLASHBACK

1 Prepare the walls thoroughly, then paint them with a rich burgundy emulsion. Stencil the anchor stencil E and compass stencil D motifs on the tiles using a silver ceramic tile or spray paint.

2 Decide on the positions of the rope and knots (stencils A and F), measuring carefully to ensure that the corners fit properly and the ropes are equidistant from the tiles.

3 As you are working on a dark background, first paint the stencils white as an undercoat for the grey paint. When dry, paint the ropes in tones of grey.

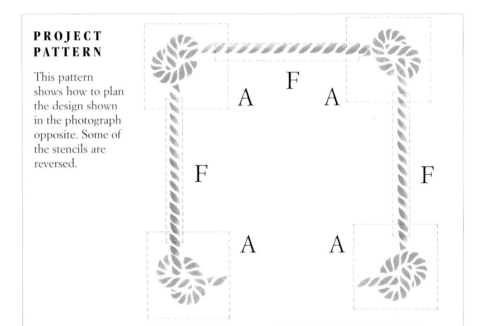

PROJECT PATTERN

This pattern shows how to plan the design shown in the photograph opposite. Some of the stencils are reversed.

LINKING THE ROPES AND KNOTS
It is most important to measure the positions of the stencils so the ropes will link together. Paint the two lengths of straight rope stencil F leaving enough space for the corner knot to fit in neatly.

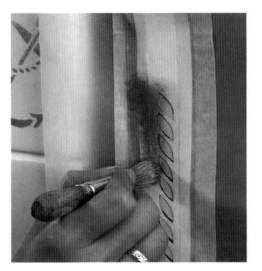

MAKING THE ROPE THREE-DIMENSIONAL
To give the rope a three-dimensional appearance, paint it darker on the side that is furthest from the light source in the room. Grey with a little black added will give you the correct tone.

MAKING THE ROPE FIT
When you are painting a repeating design into a limited space it is sometimes necessary to 'stretch' or 'squeeze' the pattern to fit. Do this by fitting a single piece of rope stencil into the space between two lengths of rope as necessary.

NAUTICAL KNOTS VARIATIONS

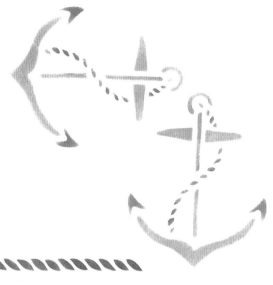

F it ropes and knots together to make borders and frames. Use stencils F and B to make a square and place a compass or anchor in the centre. Stencils A and F will make a rope hanging for a picture, and if you cover the circle on the compass with masking tape you have a star. These nautical designs look good in blue.

NAUTICAL BORDER (STENCILS D, E AND F)

ABOVE: ANCHOR CORNER (STENCIL E)

STAR SQUARE (STENCIL D)

ANCHOR TILE PATTERN (STENCIL E)

LEFT: ROPE AND KNOTS BORDER (STENCILS C AND F)

COMPASS TILE (STENCIL D)

STAR WALLPAPER DESIGN (STENCIL D)

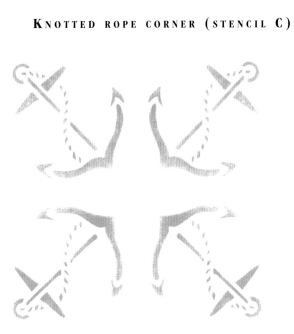

KNOTTED ROPE CORNER (STENCIL C)

ANCHOR TILES (STENCIL E)

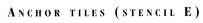

REFLECTED ANCHOR FRIEZE (STENCIL E)

ROPE PICTURE HANGER (STENCILS B AND F)

COMPASS BORDER (STENCIL D)

KNOTTED ROPE FRAME (STENCILS A AND F)

SIMPLE KNOTTED ROPE BORDER (STENCIL C)

CORAL REEF

Run the bath, pour a glass of wine, light the candles and relax in your very own tropical paradise. The gold-painted bubbles will sparkle in the candlelight. Inspired by the myriad of colourful fish that are found in the ocean around a coral reef, this bathroom is fun and easy to paint and a pleasure to live with. Why stop at the walls? Try using the stencils to decorate a blind for the window, a bathmat or the floor itself.

PAINT COLOUR GUIDE

Sea green silk emulsion	White	Orange
Deep blue-green	Red	Ultramarine
Lemon yellow	Gold spray paint	

CREATING AN UNDERSEA SCENE

1 Paint the wall with sea green silk emulsion paint. Mix a glaze using acrylic scumble and deep blue-green paint. Then, with a sponge, gently wipe the glaze over the wall to represent the waves.

2 Plan the positions of the bubbles stencil D and fish. Place similar fish in 'shoals'. Paint the fish using two or three bright colours for each type.

3 Paint the bubbles using gold spray paint. Spray lightly, gradually building up the colour to avoid paint running behind the stencil.

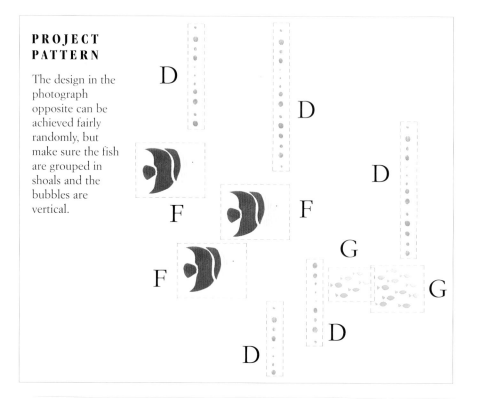

PROJECT PATTERN

The design in the photograph opposite can be achieved fairly randomly, but make sure the fish are grouped in shoals and the bubbles are vertical.

ENSURING VIBRANT COLOURS
When the background is dark it is advisable to give stencils an undercoat of white paint. This ensures that subsequent colours will be more vibrant. Leave the stencil in position and let the white dry before adding the colour. Speed up the drying with a hairdryer.

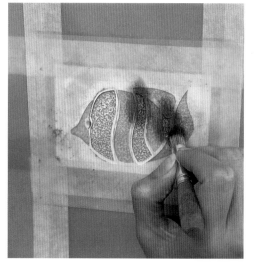

KEEPING COLOURS SEPARATE
When colours need to be kept separate, make a tracing paper mask to cover the areas not to be painted. You will need one mask for each colour you are using. Leave the stencil in position, fix the mask over it and paint through.

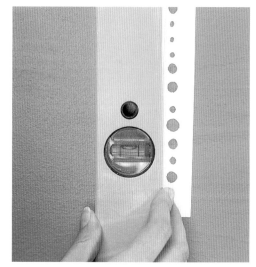

GETTING THE BUBBLES VERTICAL
To look right it is important that the bubbles are vertical on the wall, so use a spirit level or plumbline to position the stencil. Change the look by painting just a few bubbles or overlapping the stencil and adding some extra ones to the line.

CORAL REEF VARIATIONS

T he tropical fish make excellent colourful borders. Try reversing the stencils so that fish are nose to nose and tail to tail. Real fish come in a multitude of colours, so be bold and experiment with your own bright scheme! Small items may be decorated with individual stencils to co-ordinate accessories in a bathroom. You could use the bubbles stencil D to decorate a picture frame.

FISH FRIEZE (STENCILS B AND C)

ABOVE: SEA ANEMONE FRIEZE (STENCIL E)

SEA ANEMONES TILES (STENCILS D AND E)

TROPICAL FISH ARCH (STENCIL A)

BELOW: CORAL REEF BORDER (STENCIL H)

CORAL CIRCLE (STENCIL H)

RIGHT: FISH BORDER AND CORNER (STENCIL C)

Sea anemones motif (stencil E)

Right: Coral corner (stencil H)

Kissing fish border (stencil B)

Kissing fish border (stencil A)

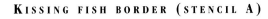

Sea anemones cluster (stencil E)

Below: Fish border (stencil F)

Shoal of small fish (stencil G)

Below: Fish and bubbles border (stencils D and F)

Bubble starburst (stencil D)

ROCK POOLS

Sitting on the patio, this urn shimmers beautifully in the sunlight. It is stencilled in soft pinks and peaches, topped with a gold rim, and the iridescent colours catch the light. Seaweed winds its way around the pot and sea creatures hide in the fronds. You may need a little practice to paint on curved surfaces, but the technique is easily mastered. If your urn is made from papier mâché, as this is, remember not to leave it outside in inclement weather.

PAINT COLOUR GUIDE

Cream	Iridescent orange	Red
Iridescent pink	Sugar pink	Gold acrylic

DECORATING AN URN

1 Paint the urn with two coats of cream emulsion. Do not paint the gold rim until all the stencilling is complete.

2 Use oil sticks for this project, so try blending the colours for interesting effects. For instance, the crab (stencil A) works well painted orange and edged with red.

3 Space the motifs around the urn so that they are evenly distributed. Take care when working with oil sticks as handling can cause smudges. Leave the oil colours to dry for a day before varnishing the urn to protect it.

PROJECT PATTERN

The stencils in the photograph opposite are arranged at random to meander around the contours of the urn.

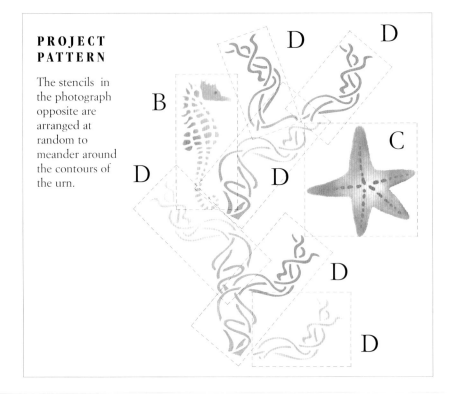

PLACING THE SEAWEED
Paint the first length of seaweed (stencil D). Then use masking tape to block out part of the stencil and position it so a further piece of weed appears to be growing from the first piece of seaweed. In this way the fronds can be extended to any length.

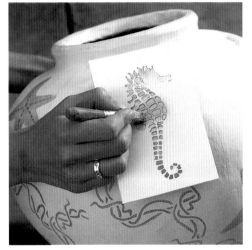

WORKING AROUND THE URN
When working on a curved surface it is not possible to keep the stencil completely flat. Hold the stencil so that the area you are painting is in contact with the urn and move it around the curve as necessary.

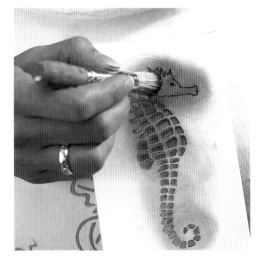

INNER STENCIL DETAILS
The details such as the eye of the seahorse or the marks on the starfish are added by using the inner stencil. Paint the seahorse and without moving the stencil fit the head piece into position. Use a slightly darker colour to paint the eye.

ROCK POOL VARIATIONS

These stencils can be used singly or in combinations and give an exciting range of possibilities. The seahorse is a delightful decoration for a frame and the seaweed makes an undulating border. Painting the stencils with at least two colours gives depth and form to the shapes – the crab would look less imposing without shading at the edge of its shell. These stencils would combine well with many of the other stencils in the book.

LINKED SEAHORSE FRAMING (STENCIL B)

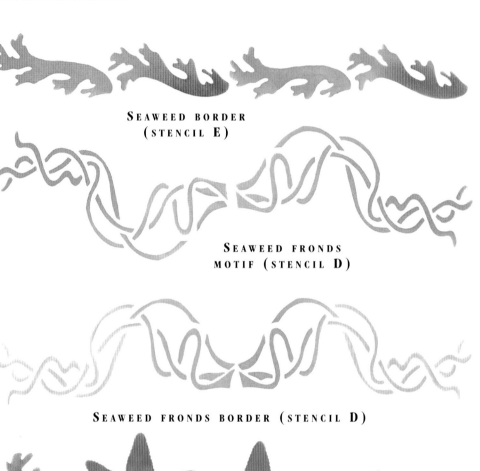

SEAWEED BORDER (STENCIL E)

SEAWEED FRONDS MOTIF (STENCIL D)

SEAWEED FRONDS BORDER (STENCIL D)

VERTICAL CRAB BORDER (STENCIL A)

STARFISH TILE (STENCIL C)

CRABS ON THE MARCH BORDER (STENCIL A)

LEFT: SEAWEED CORNER (STENCIL E)

ABOVE: SEAWEED BORDER (STENCIL E)

LEFT: SEAWEED CLUMP (STENCIL E)

ABOVE: SEAWEED FRONDS CORNER (STENCIL D)

STARFISH WITH BUBBLES (STENCILS C AND 'CORAL REEF' STENCIL D)

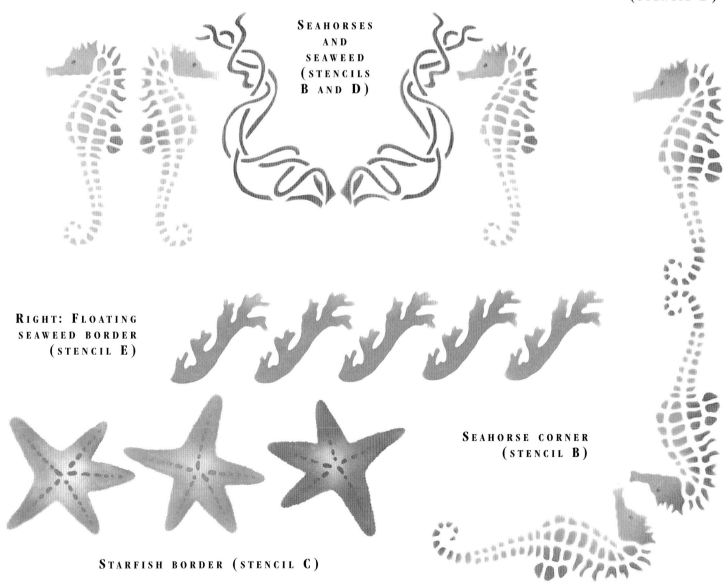

SEAHORSES AND SEAWEED (STENCILS B AND D)

RIGHT: FLOATING SEAWEED BORDER (STENCIL E)

SEAHORSE CORNER (STENCIL B)

STARFISH BORDER (STENCIL C)

SUPPLIERS

Emulsion paints are easily obtainable from DIY stores and good hardware stores; contact manufacturers below for your nearest supplier. Oil sticks and acrylic paints can be obtained from artists' materials stores. Other stencilling supplies can usually be found in any of the above and there are many dedicated stencil stores.

Imperial Chemical Industries plc
(ICI)
(Dulux paints)
Wexham Road
Slough
SL2 5DS
(Tel. 01753 550000)

Crown Decorative Products
PO Box 37
Crown House
Hollins Road
Darwen
Lancashire
(Tel. 01254 704951)

Fired Earth plc
Twyford Mill
Oxford Road
Adderbury
Oxfordshire
(Tel. 01295 812088)

ACKNOWLEDGEMENTS

Merehurst wish to thank the following for their help: Dulux Advice Centre; The Pier; BHS; The Home Place; The Water Monopoly.

First published in 1998 by Merehurst Limited
Ferry House, 51–57 Lacy Road, Putney, London SW15 1PR

ISBN 1-85391-726-5

A catalogue record of this book is available from the British Library.

Commissioning Editor: Karen Hemingway
Introductory text: Julie Collins
Editor: Geraldine Christy
Designer: Roger Hammond
Photographer: Graeme Ainscough
Stylist: Caroline Davis

CEO & Publisher: Anne Wilson
International Sales Director: Mark Newman

Colour separation by Bright Arts (HK) Limited
Printed in Singapore

Denise Westcott Taylor teaches stencilling and paint effects courses as well as taking on private commissions. She is also currently teaching a City and Guilds course on working designs for creative studies.